ADVENTURES IN NATURE

POND WILDLIFE

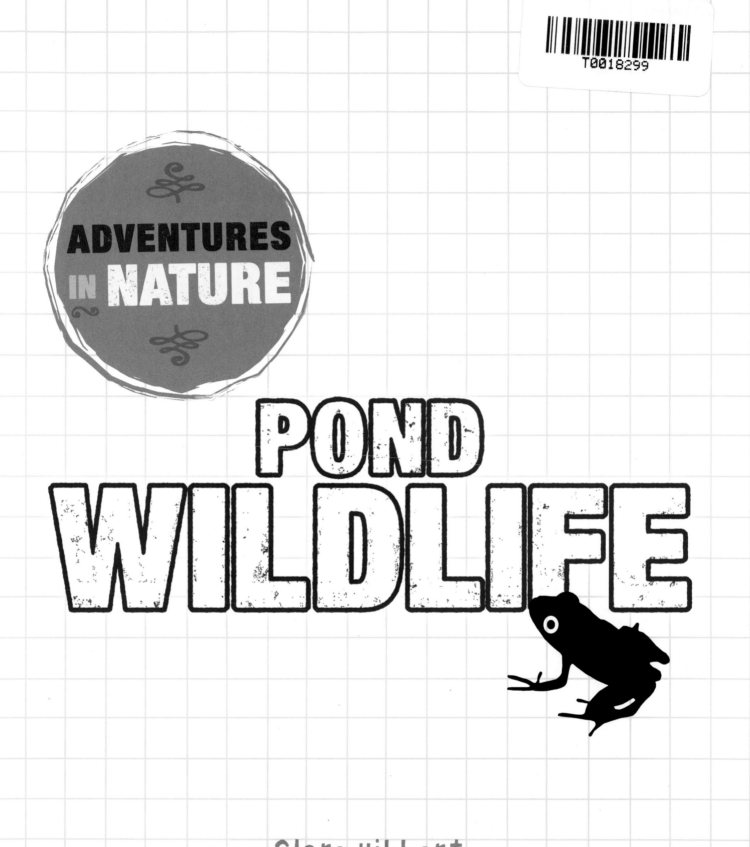

Clare Hibbert

PowerKiDS press

Published in 2016 by
The Rosen Publishing Group, Inc.
29 East 21st Street, New York, NY 10010

Cataloging-in-Publication Data
Hibbert, Clare.
Pond wildlife / by Clare Hibbert.
p. cm. — (Adventures in nature)
Includes index.
ISBN 978-1-5081-4587-5 (pbk.)
ISBN 978-1-5081-4588-2 (6-pack)
ISBN 978-1-5081-4589-9 (library binding)
1. Ponds — Juvenile literature. 2. Pond ecology — Juvenile
literature. 3. Pond animals — Juvenile literature.
I. Hibbert, Clare, 1970-. II. Title.
QH98.H53 2016
551.48'2—d23

Copyright © 2016 Watts/PowerKids

Series Editor: Sarah Peutrill
Series Designer: Matt Lilly
Picture Researcher: Kathy Lockley
Illustrations: Andy Elkerton

Picture Credits: Dreamstime.com/Alex Scott 11TC, 15b,
Andybignellphoto 27TR, Bobbrooky 23C, Bombaert 7d,
Catalinc 10T, Chonlawut Brahmasakha 15CL, Darius Bauzys
11TL, David734244 15C, Dfikar 27BR, Dirk Ercken 8TR, Elena
Duvernay 25b, Ginger Sanders 5e, Gow927 28T, Hwongcc
15d, Iperl 7b, Isselee Contents page B, 19T, Jnjhuz 25g,
25d, Johncarnemolla 24, Jolanta Dabrowska 23L, 23R, Joloei
15a, Kamionka 20T, Kazakov Maksim 23c, Lin Whitehead 7a,
Lukas Blazek 21d, Mariusz Prusaczyk 23a, Mauro77photo 5d,
Mgkuijpers 21b, Michael Adams 27CR, Michael Wood Contents
page C, 16T, 17BL, Natashak 7BR, Orionmystery Contents
page T, 11ACR, 13TR, Outdoorsman 27TL, Paul Reeves 25a,
Peter Zijlstra 23b, Robert Taylor 29f, Rudmer Zwerver 27CL,
Sashoilievski 5f, Somchai Rak-in 15e, Sommaiphoto 15L, Steve
Byland 21a, Steve Guest 5a, Suyerry 29c, Szefei 11BC, Viter8
11TR, Vluggevogel 27b, Vyacheslav Pylypenko 6, Wasana
Jaigunta 15c, Whiskybottle 10B, Wisconsinart 15R, Witr 29b,
Zhitao Li 11BCR; iStockphoto.com/Andy-Holt 11AC; FLPA/Alwyn
J. Roberts 16B, Nigel Cattlin 13TC, Photo Researchers 20B;
Photoshot/Stephen Dalton/NHPA 11BR, Stephen Dalton/Ocenas-
Image 8BL; Shutterstock.com/alle 11BL, Andrew Skolnick 9C,
Arseniy Krasnevsky 5c, Artur Synenko 18, Avurus 4B, BMJ
15BR, Chris Hill 26B, CrazyStocker 17R, drsuth48 25e and h,
Eduard Kyslynskyy 27C, Eric Isselee 9TR, 13CR, Erni 19BR,
26T, Hector Ruiz Villar 8TL, 29a, Infomages 7c, Jamie Hooper
5b, Jay Ondreicka 21c, Jiang Hongyan 13C, mstepanov 15CR,
Myper Front Cover, Olexandr Taranukhin 23BL,d Olga Phoenix
9BL, pan demin 12B, Paul Sparks 29d, Pavelk 14, Phoric 23CR,
sakhorn 12T, sciencepics 13CL, Sergey Goruppa 17LC, Steven
Frame 27ACR, StevenRussellSmithPhotos 17TC, Sue Robinson
4T, 9TC, val lawless 28B, Vishnevskiy Vasily 22, Vitalii Hulai 9BR,
9TL, Willequet Manuel 25 c and f; US Fish & Wildlife Service/
Adult striped newt by Kevin M. Enge, Florida Fish & Wildlife
Conservation Commission

Manufactured in the United States of America

CPSIA Compliance Information: Batch #BW16PK: For Further Information contact
Rosen Publishing, New York, New York at 1-800-237-9932

Can you find SIX red dragonflies hidden on the pages?

Stay safe around ponds

If you are going near the edge, make sure an adult is near. The water can be deep, cold, or difficult to get out of. It might contain hidden rubbish or pollution that could injure you or make you ill.

Clara is out looking for pond creatures. Can you find her?

There are lots more puzzles in this book. You can solve them by reading the text or by looking closely at the photos. The answers are on page 30.

Contents

The great pond hunt

A pond is home to lots of different wildlife. It is a small, self-contained world known as a microhabitat. Ponds contain fresh water, so the animals and plants that live in or around them need to be suited to life in or around fresh water.

Water striders are insects that live on ponds.

Pond water does not rush along like the water in a stream or river. It is usually still (not moving). It may just be rainwater that has filled a dip in the land. Sometimes ponds are fed by a small stream or by an underground spring where water gently bubbles up. In these ponds, there is slow-moving water.

There are ponds all over the world, except at the North and South Poles.

ponds or imposters?

Look at these watery places. Can you tell which are ponds? What other watery habitats can you see?

a

b

c

d

e

f

THE pond HUNT CHALLENGE

Pond spotting

Visit your local pond. How many different birds and other animals can you spot in one hour?

Types of ponds

Ponds come in many shapes and sizes. They can be shallow or deep, have steep sides or sloping ones. Some of them are natural, but many are artificial ponds that people have made. These are called ornamental ponds. People like to see them in gardens and parks because they are so beautiful and calming. People choose pretty plants and colorful fish to put in these ornamental ponds – but wild species soon arrive, too!

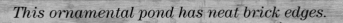

This ornamental pond has neat brick edges.

Spot the seasons

Ponds look very different in different seasons. Can you figure out the season for each picture – spring, summer, autumn, or winter?

Pesky visitors

Some ponds contain expensive plants and fish. Koi carp belong to the goldfish family and have beautiful white, gold, and black markings. They cost a lot of money – but hungry cats and big birds called herons don't care about that! Pond keepers have to find ways to stop these predators from catching the fish.

Koi carp have pretty markings.

Bugs

larva (young) of a great diving beetle

great diving beetle

All sorts of bugs live in the pond. It can be hard to tell which are insects. Adult insects have six legs, but insect babies often look nothing like their parents. The names can be confusing, too. Despite their name, water fleas are crustaceans, not insects. They are related to prawns, not fleas!

diving-bell spider with its air bubble

Insects that hunt in the water include water scorpions, water boatmen, and great diving beetles. On the surface, water striders (see page 4) and whirligig beetles scuttle and spin. One of the best hunters is a spider, not an insect. The diving-bell spider lives underwater attached to a bubble of air.

Name the creatures

There are six pond creatures here, but the letters of their names are all jumbled up. Can you unscramble the names to identify them? Can you tell which are insects?

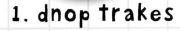

1. dnop trakes

2. atrew procnosi

5. smirkwemcab

4. tager givnid leteeb

3. teraw dripes

6. trawe kicts tensic

THE pond HUNT CHALLENGE

Pond dipping

Go pond dipping with an adult. See how many creatures you can identify!

Pond dipping is a great way to see pond life up close, but only do it when an adult is with you. You will need a net to sweep up creatures and a clean white tub in which to put your finds while you look at them (always put them back in the pond afterwards). Look online for species checklists (see page 32) to help you identify what you find.

pond fliers

Dragonflies and damselflies are insects that hunt above the surface of the water. These powerful fliers speed through the air after gnats, midges, and other flying insects. However, they spend the early part of their life underwater. To lay her eggs without getting her wings wet, a female dragonfly lowers her tail down a pond plant stem. The eggs hatch into dragonfly larvae (young).

Damselflies are smaller and slimmer than dragonflies.

This dragonfly is laying her eggs underwater.

Whose baby?

Dragonflies and damselflies aren't the only flying insects that live in the pond when they are babies. Match these adults to their young by unjumbling the labels.

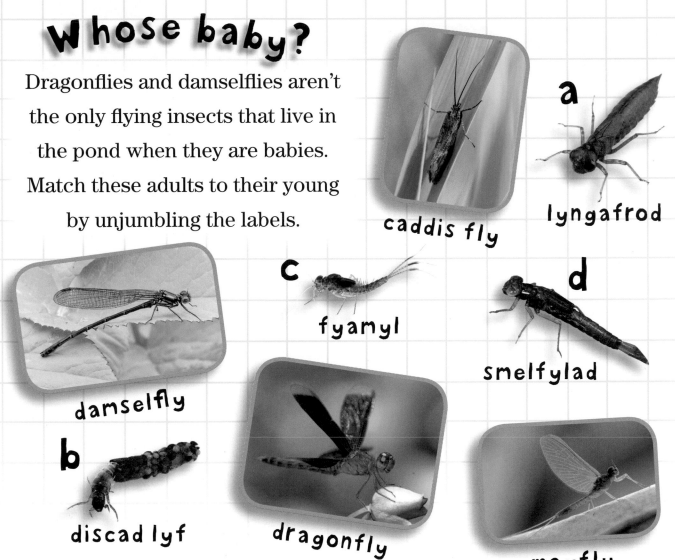

caddis fly

a
lyngafrod

c
fyamyl

d
smelfylad

damselfly

b
discad lyf

dragonfly

mayfly

Scary babies

Dragonfly larvae are fierce hunters, armed with large pincers and a spiked lower lip for snatching prey. They hunt other larvae, tadpoles, and even small fish. As they grow, they molt (shed their skin). The final molt happens at the surface. An adult dragonfly crawls out, complete with brand-new wings!

This dragonfly larva has caught a fish.

Slimy creatures

Freshwater snails live in the pond. They graze on algae and plants. They lay their eggs in long strings, attached to the underside of leaves. When the baby snails hatch, they have a ready supply of food. Snails are a kind of mollusk, with a shell to protect their soft, slimy body. Freshwater clams are mollusks, too. They sieve scraps of food from the water.

Pond snails lay their eggs on a plant stem.

The leech's sucker is on its underside.

The muddy bottom of the pond is home to flatworms, redworms, and other wriggly creatures. Leeches belong to the same family as earthworms. They have suckers to slurp up rotting bodies or to suck blood from fish, frogs, and other animals.

Which slimeball?

Here are some slimy creatures that live in freshwater ponds. Can you match each one to its outline?

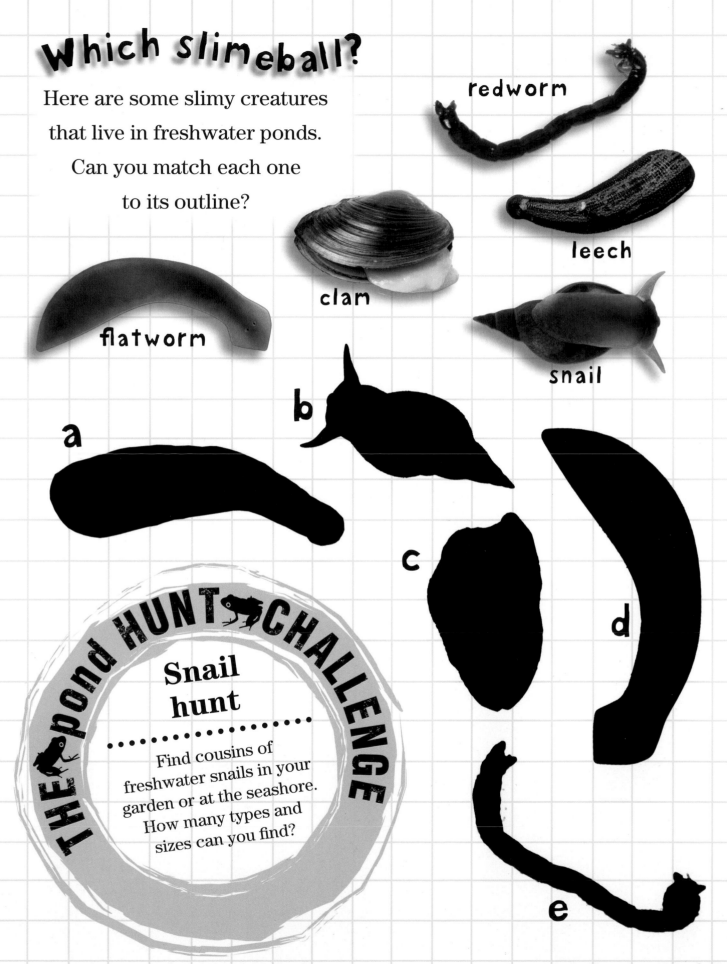

redworm

leech

clam

snail

flatworm

b

a

c

d

e

THE pond HUNT CHALLENGE

Snail hunt

Find cousins of freshwater snails in your garden or at the seashore. How many types and sizes can you find?

All kinds of plants

Ponds are home to many kinds of plants. Underwater ones often have feathery, frond-like leaves. Plants on the surface have shiny leaves that the water can run off. The tiny, bright green leaves that often cover the surface of a pond are duckweed. Water soldier also floats, but it sinks to the bottom after flowering and stays there till the following spring.

water lilies

Plants live at all levels of the pond.

pond plants

Look closely at these plant parts. Which plants do they come from?

a   b   c   d   e

water hyacinth   mosquito fern   duckweed   violet   algae

How plants make food

Like land plants, aquatic plants and algae make their own food. Their magic ingredient is the chlorophyll that makes them green. This chemical mixes sunlight, carbon dioxide (a gas from the air), and water to produce sugar. The process is called photosynthesis. Some pond plants also get extra nutrients by trapping tiny creatures!

Bladderwort sucks tiny creatures into its traps and then digests them.

15

Freshwater fish

There are lots of different types of freshwater fish. Some are happiest in rivers and streams. Others, such as carp, rudd, and sticklebacks, prefer the stiller water of a pond. Larger fish need deeper water, so the bigger the pond, the larger the fish that can live there.

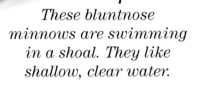

These bluntnose minnows are swimming in a shoal. They like shallow, clear water.

Male sticklebacks make nests to protect the eggs.

Fish reproduce by laying eggs. The eggs hatch into young fish, called fry. Fry are a tasty mouthful, so fish lay their eggs in the shallows, where big predators cannot come. Sticklebacks tunnel out a nest on the bottom of the pond for their eggs. The male stickleback fans the eggs with his fins, bringing them oxygenated water.

Fishy foods

Each of these fish is matched to an outline of its favorite food. Can you guess the name of each food from the list on the right?

chironomid larvae   bluegill   crayfish   pond snail

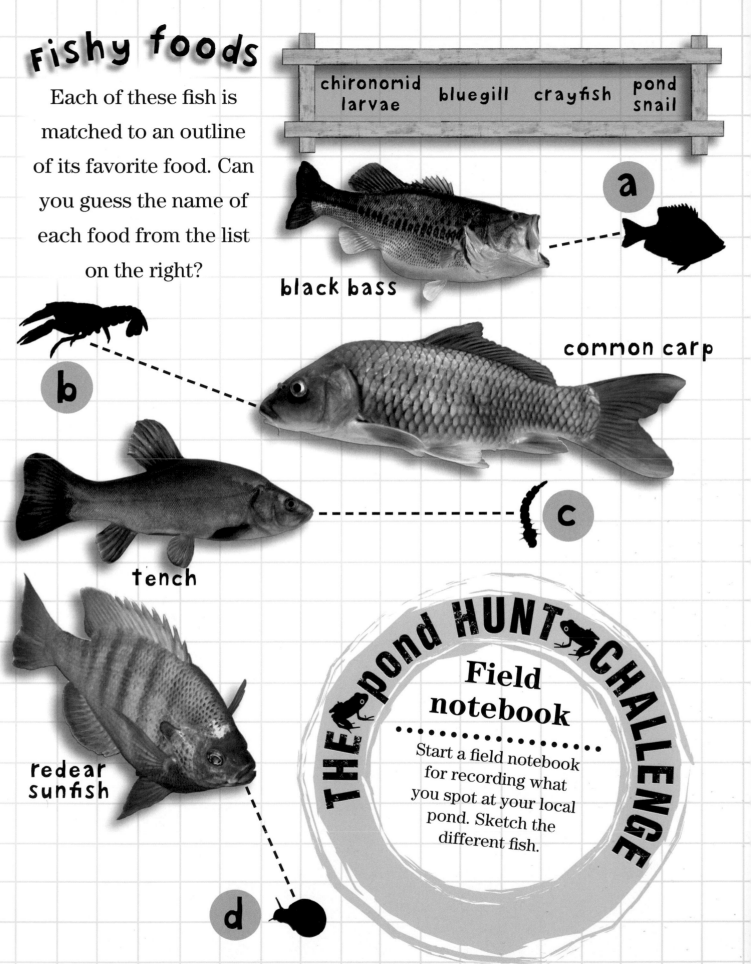

a

black bass

b

common carp

c

tench

redear sunfish

d

THE pond HUNT CHALLENGE

Field notebook

Start a field notebook for recording what you spot at your local pond. Sketch the different fish.

Frogs

Frogs belong to a family of slimy-skinned animals called amphibians. They spend part of their life in water and part on land. Adult frogs lay jelly-like eggs called frogspawn in the pond. These eggs hatch into tadpoles. The tadpoles look nothing like adult frogs – they have a tail, no legs, and they breathe through gills. As they grow, they lose their tail, grow legs, and develop lungs.

An adult frog on a lily pad

From egg to frog

These pictures (a to f) show the different stages in the life cycle of a frog. Can you put them in the right order?

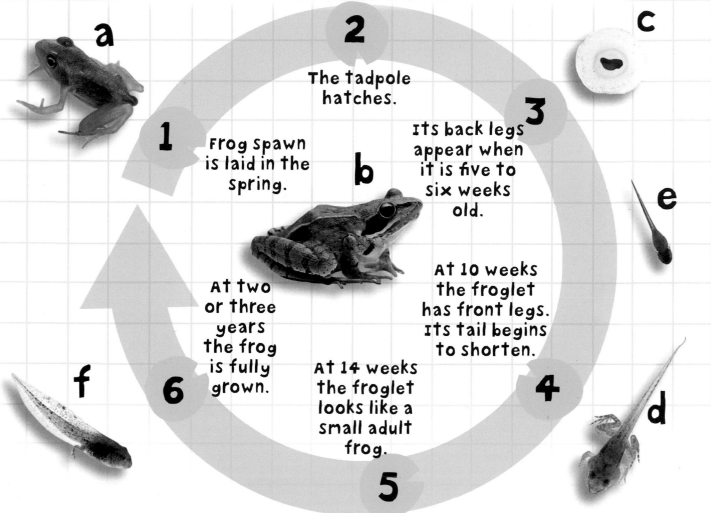

a

c

e

b

f

d

2 The tadpole hatches.

1 Frog spawn is laid in the spring.

3 Its back legs appear when it is five to six weeks old.

4 At 10 weeks the froglet has front legs. Its tail begins to shorten.

6 At two or three years the frog is fully grown.

5 At 14 weeks the froglet looks like a small adult frog.

More amphibians

Toads and salamanders are amphibians too, and they also live in the pond. Toads have wartier skin than frogs and they lay their eggs in long strings. Salamanders have longer, thinner bodies and they keep their tails as adults. Newts are a kind of salamander.

A common newt swims through pondweed.

19

Pond reptiles

Snakes are reptiles – scaly-skinned animals that cannot make their own body heat. Grass snakes and water snakes hunt for frogs and fish in ponds. They are good swimmers. Snakes are very shy, so it is rare to see one. If you are lucky, you might see the papery skin left behind by a snake when it molted.

grass snake

In some parts of the world, ponds are home to other kinds of reptile, including freshwater turtles, lizards, and even alligators! The extraordinary basilisk lizard lives in Central and South America. If it needs to escape a predator, it is light enough to race across a pond or stream.

This young striped basilisk is running across the surface of the water.

pond turtles

These freshwater turtles all live in North America. Look closely at the pictures. Can you figure out their names?

1. smooth softshell turtle
2. yellow-bellied turtle
3. spotted turtle
4. alligator snapping turtle

a

b

c

d

THE pond HUNT CHALLENGE

Snake spotting

Next time you are near a pond, see if you can spot a papery snake skin.

Life on the edge

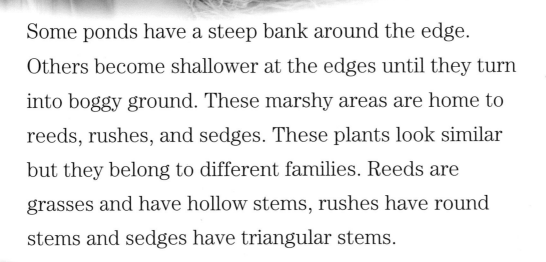

Reed warblers build their nests among the reeds.

Some ponds have a steep bank around the edge. Others become shallower at the edges until they turn into boggy ground. These marshy areas are home to reeds, rushes, and sedges. These plants look similar but they belong to different families. Reeds are grasses and have hollow stems, rushes have round stems and sedges have triangular stems.

Fringe flowers

Plants that live by the pond are called marginal plants because they are around its margins (edges). Can you match the right flowerheads to these marginal plants?

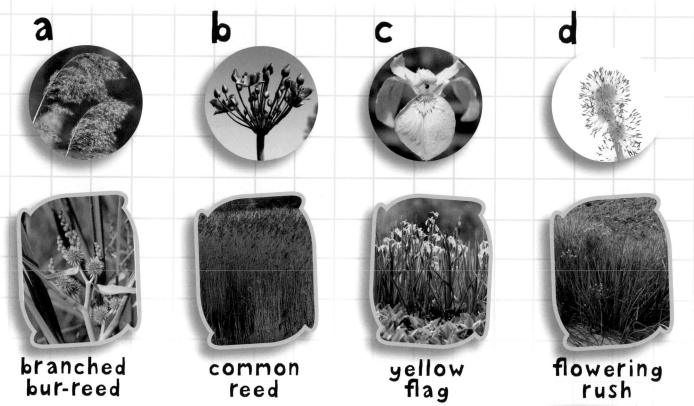

a **b** **c** **d**

branched bur-reed **common reed** **yellow flag** **flowering rush**

Sundews

sundew →

Sundews are strange, carnivorous plants that live by ponds. Carnivorous means "meat-eating," and the "meat" that sundews "eat" comes from insects. Sundews attract their prey by producing blobs of sweet, sticky liquid. The blobs look like harmless drops of dew but they trap the insects so they cannot escape.

pond birds

This grey heron has caught a young frog.

Small birds such as reed buntings and reed warblers nest by the pond. Buntings build their tiny nests on the ground, but warblers weave theirs between the reed stems (see page 22). These birds feed on insects and seeds. Ducks and other water birds also nest among the reeds or along the banks.

Moorhens prefer to build reed platforms that float in the water. Water birds spend the day swimming on the surface of the pond and diving for plants, snails, and fish to eat. Kingfishers, herons, and storks have a different hunting technique – they stand on the bank for hours and then suddenly spear a fish or a frog.

Mr. and Mrs.

Male ducks often have much showier feathers than females. See if you can match each male and female pair.

a

female

b

male

c

male

d

female

e

male

f

female

g

male

h

female

THE pond HUNT CHALLENGE

Collect feathers

Next time you are at a pond, wear gloves to collect beautiful feathers left by water birds.

Furry creatures

Voles, shrews, water rats, and muskrats are mammals that build their burrows on the banks of the pond. The burrows have their main entrance underwater, safe from predators. Water voles feed on reeds and rushes. Water shrews and water rats are hunters. They catch freshwater shrimps, insects, frogs, newts, and small fish in the pond. They also hunt worms, snails and beetles on land.

Water shrews are tiny – less than 4 inches (10 cm) long.

Muskrats like this one eat plants and small animals.

Who's who?

Mammals hunt by sight, smell, and sound. See if you can match the close-up eyes, noses, and ears to their owners.

a

b

c

d

e

f

fox

water vole

water shrew

opossum

muskrat

wildcat

Beaver ponds

Beavers don't live in ponds – they make them! These big rodents live in rivers and lakes. They cut down trees and other plants, which they use to build homes and dams. The dams create beaver ponds, where the beavers can store wood and other plant foods.

Beavers have powerful front teeth for cutting wood.

Changing ponds

This man is removing some of the plants from an overcrowded pond.

Ponds change with the seasons (see page 7). Over longer time spans, they change in other ways. If a pond does not have enough predators, it will become overcrowded. If it does not contain enough plant-eaters, its plants and algae will grow out of control and the water will turn murky and green.

This pond has started to dry up because of lack of rain.

Sometimes pond wildlife has to cope with more serious issues. If pollution washes into ponds it can harm or kill the wildlife. If a pond becomes polluted or overcrowded, people can clean it up and encourage a good balance of plants and animals.

Disappearing wildlife

Many pond species are in danger of dying out. People are working to save all of these endangered pond animals – can you match each one to the right name?

1 great crested newt

2 Aylesbury duck

3 natterjack toad

4 thin emerald dragonfly

5 striped newt

6 carolina gopher frog

a

b

c

d

e

f

THE pond HUNT CHALLENGE

Save a pond

With an adult, find out if you can help to clear out a local pond.

Puzzle answers

5 Pond or imposters?

ponds: b, f
imposters: a, c, d, e
Other habitats: rockpool (a);
river (c); lake (d); puddle (e).

7 Spot the seasons

spring – d
summer – b
autumn – c
winter – a

9 Name the creatures

1 – pond skater
2 – water scorpion
3 – water spider
4 – great diving beetle
5 – backswimmer
6 – water stick insect

Insects: they are all insects
except for the water spider.
(The water scorpion might
have tricked you because its
front legs look like pincers,
for grabbing prey but they
are actually legs.)

11 Whose baby?

caddis fly – b
damselfly – d
dragonfly – a
mayfly – c

13 Which slimeball?

redworm – e
flatworm – d
clam – c
leech – a
snail – b

15 Pond plants

a – algae
b – water hyacinth
c – mosquito fern
d – violet
e – duckweed

17 Fishy foods

a – bluegill
b – crayfish
c – chironomid larvae
d – pond snail

19 From egg to frog

1 – c; 2 – e; 3 – f; 4 – d;
5 – a; 6 – b.

21 Pond turtles

a – 3; b – 1;
c – 2; d – 4.

23 Fringe flowers

a – common reed
b – flowering rush
c – yellow flag
d – branched bur-reed

25 Mr. and Mrs.

c and f – mallards
g and a – goldeneyes
b and d – goosanders
e and h – cinnamon teal

27 Who's who?

a – muskrat
b – fox
c – wildcat
d – opossum
e – water vole
f – water shrew

29 Disappearing wildlife

a – 3; b – 1; c – 6; d – 4;
e – 5; f – 2

Glossary

alga (pl. algae) A plant-like living thing that grows in water. Like plants, algae make their own food using photosynthesis.

amphibian An animal with a bony skeleton and slimy skin that lives partly on land, partly in the water, and cannot make its own body heat.

aquatic Living or growing in a water environment.

artificial Made by people; not natural.

carnivorous Meat-eating.

chlorophyll A green chemical in plants and algae that takes in energy from sunlight.

fry Young fish that have just hatched.

gill One of a pair of feathery body parts that allow aquatic animals to take oxygen from water.

habitat A place where animals and plants live in the wild.

larva (pl. larvae) The young stage of an animal, usually an insect, that looks nothing like its parent.

life cycle All the different stages in the life of a living thing.

mammal An animal with a bony skeleton and fur or hair that can make its own body heat and feeds its babies milk.

marginal From or growing around the edge.

microhabitat A self-contained environment where animals and plants live.

mollusk A boneless animal with a soft body that needs to be kept damp and is sometimes protected by a shell.

molt Lose skin, hair or an outer casing.

nutrient Goodness that feeds an animal or plant.

oxygenated Full of oxygen, the gas in air and water that all animals need to breathe.

photosynthesis The way plants and algae make food energy when their chlorophyll reacts with sunlight, carbon dioxide and water to make sugars.

pollution Damage to the environment caused by the actions of human beings. Chemicals that run off farmers' fields into ponds pollute the water.

predator An animal that hunts other animals for food.

prey An animal that is hunted by other animals for food.

reproduce Produce offspring (babies).

reptile An animal with a bony skeleton and scaly skin that cannot make its own body heat.

shoal The name for a group of fish

species One particular type of living thing. Members of the same species look like each other and can reproduce together.

spring A place where water bubbles up from between rocks in the earth. Some springs provide the water for ponds.

Index

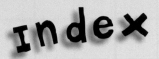

Websites

PowerKids Press has developed an online list of websites related to the subject of this book. This site is updated regularly. Please use this link to access the list:
www.powerkidslinks.com/ain/pond